th

# SPIDER

Words that look like **this** can be found in the glossary on page 24.

©2018
Book Life
King's Lynn
Norfolk PE30 4LS

ISBN: 978-1-78637-237-6

Written by:
Holly Duhig
Edited by:
Kirsty Holmes
Designed by:
Danielle Jones

A catalogue record for this book
is available from the British Library.

# SPIDER

# WHAT IS A LIFE CYCLE?

All animals, plants and humans go through different stages of their life as they grow and change. This is called a life cycle.

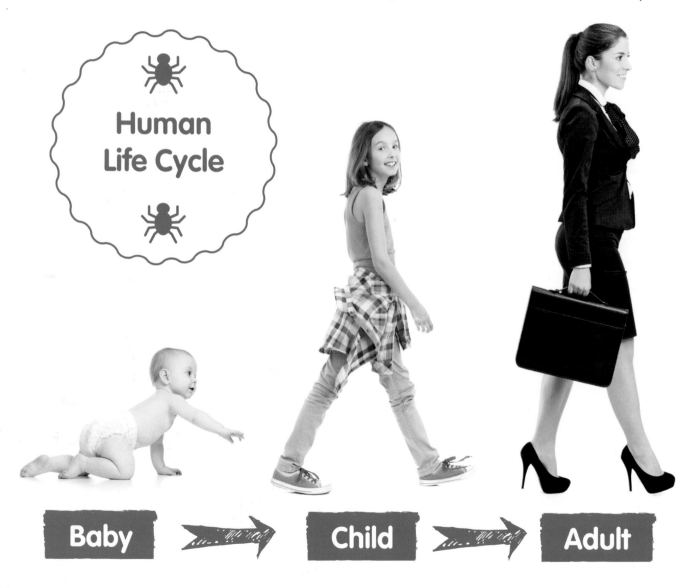

Human Life Cycle

Baby ➤➤ Child ➤➤ Adult

# WHAT IS A SPIDER?

A spider is an **arachnid**. They have eight legs and a body made of two **segments**. Their bodies make silk, which they use to build webs.

Spider

Spider Web

# EGGS

A female spider usually lays her eggs in spring. She wraps her eggs in a **sac** made of silk to protect them from **predators**.

Egg Sac

A single egg sac may be home to just a few eggs, or a few hundred! This is because different spider **species** lay different numbers of eggs.

Female spiders are usually much larger than males.

# SPIDERLINGS

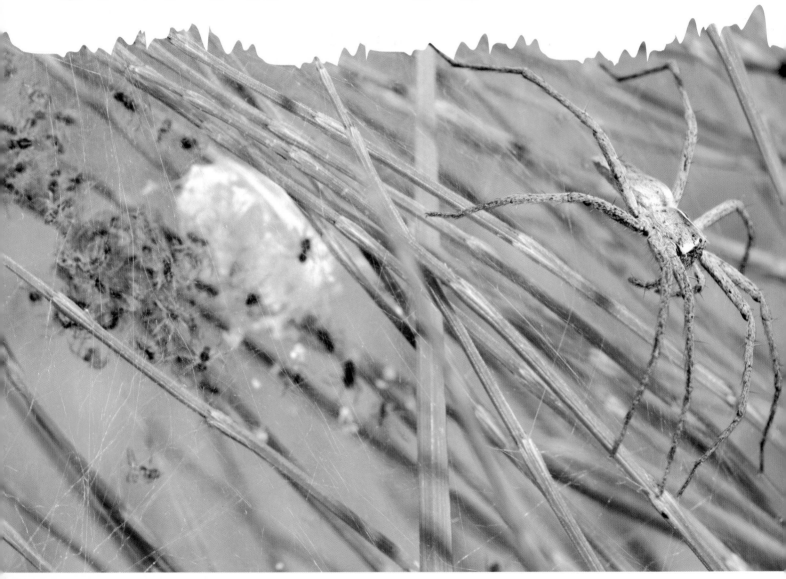

After a few weeks, the eggs will hatch. Young spiders, called spiderlings, will crawl their way out of the egg sac.

Before they hatch, spiderlings feed themselves by eating the **yolk** inside their egg. After hatching, they must learn to hunt for insects.

Spiderlings

Some spiderlings stay close to their mother once they have hatched. The female wolf spider carries her spiderlings on her back for ten days after they hatch.

**Can you count the spiderlings?**

Some spiderlings do something called 'ballooning'. This is where they shoot silk into the air which catches the wind and allows them to be blown away from their mother.

# GROWING SPIDERLINGS

A Spider Moulting

As the spiderlings grow, they shed their hard outer layer, called an **exoskeleton**, over and over again. This is called moulting.

After moulting, a spiderling's body is very weak. However, they don't stay like this for long because a bigger, harder exoskeleton begins growing straight away.

Most spiders moult between five to ten times as they grow.

# SPIDERS

Spiders never get caught in their own web because they move across it on non-sticky threads.

Adult spiders live in webs which they use to catch their **prey**. Spiders make their webs with a sticky silk, which traps insects that fly into it.

Adult female spiders begin looking for a **mate** so they can lay eggs of their own. Male jumping spiders have bright colours and long hair to attract females.

Male Jumping Spider

# SCARY SPIDERS

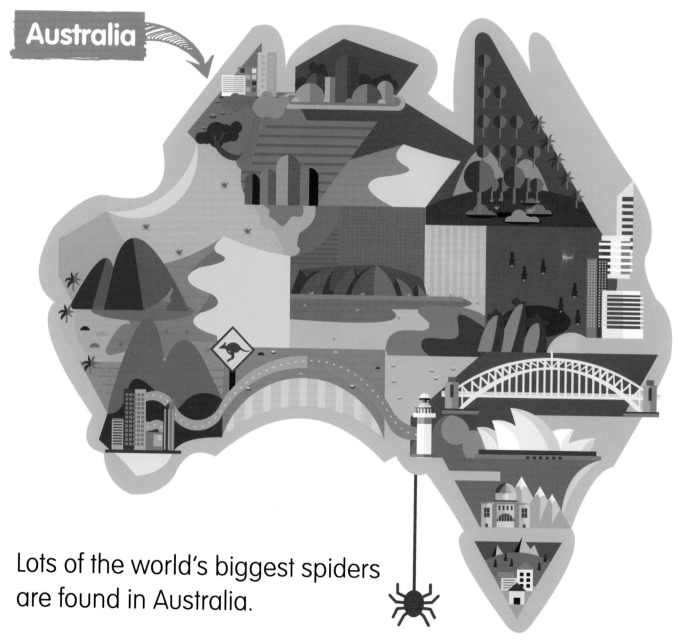

Australia

Lots of the world's biggest spiders
are found in Australia.

Fear of spiders is called arachnophobia.

# LOOKING FOR FOOD

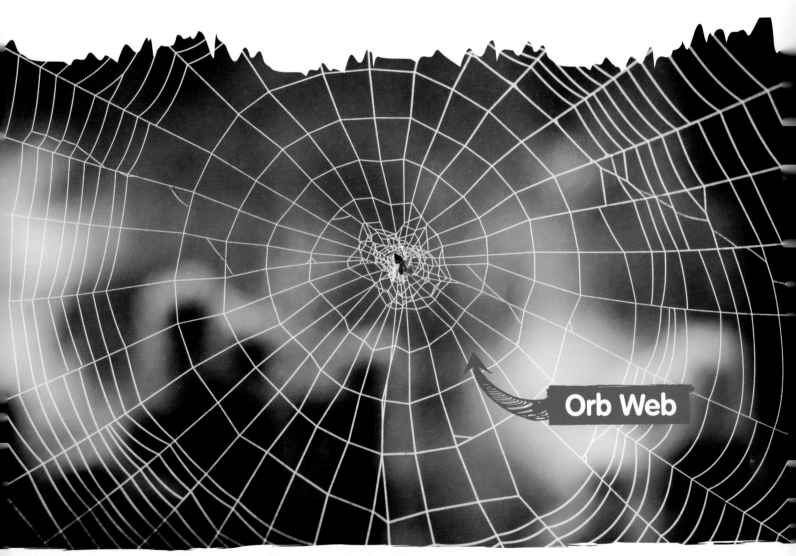

Orb Web

In an orb web, all the threads are connected. This means that when an insect touches it the whole web shakes, and the spider knows it has caught its prey.

Funnel webs are often built between tree branches or blades of grass. The web's owner waits for insects to get caught in the web's sticky sides.

Funnel Web

# WORLD RECORD BREAKERS

## Largest Spider

The largest spider ever found was a Goliath bird-eating spider. Its leg span was 28 centimetres wide. That's about the size of a dinner plate!

Goliath Bird-Eating Spider

Sydney Funnel-Web Spider

Most spiders are harmless, but some can kill!
The record for the most **venomous** spider is held by the male
Sydney funnel-web spider.

# LIFE CYCLE OF A SPIDER

**1** A female spider lays her eggs.

**2** The eggs hatch and spiderlings come out.

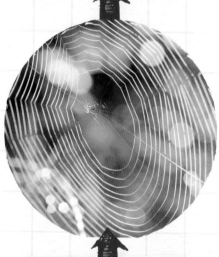

**LIFE CYCLES**

The adult spiders build their own webs. **4**

**3** The spiderlings moult until they are fully grown.

# GET EXPLORING!

Spiders live all over the place, but lots of spiders make their webs in dark places like sheds and attics. Why not see if you can find some?

# GLOSSARY

| | |
|---|---|
| **arachnid** | a class of creatures that all have eight legs, such as spiders |
| **exoskeleton** | hard structure on the outside of a creature |
| **mate** | a partner (of the same species) who an animal chooses to produce young with |
| **predators** | animals that hunt other animals for food |
| **prey** | animals that are hunted by other animals for food |
| **sac** | something a spider makes that looks like a bag or pouch |
| **segments** | parts or sections of an animal's body |
| **species** | a group of very similar animals or plants that are capable of producing young together |
| **venomous** | capable of injecting venom through a bite or a sting |
| **yolk** | the part of an egg that contains nutrients |

# INDEX

## PHOTO CREDITS

Photocredits: Abbreviations: l-left, r-right, b-bottom, t-top, c-centre, m-middle.
Front Cover —praphab louilarpprasert. 1 – praphab louilarpprasert. 2 – trangk. 3t – Matteo photos. 3m – thatmacroguy. 3b – Aleksey Stemmer. 4l – Oksana Kuzmina. 4m – studioloco. 4r – Ljupco Smokovski. 5 – FloridaStock. 6 – Iurochkin Alexandr. 7 – Eric Isselee. 8 – Marco Maggesi. 9 – Kletr. 10 – Sean McVey. 11 – NataBene. 12l&r – Perry chang. 13 – Noppharat616. 14 – Pascale Gueret. 15 – Marek Velechovsky. 17t – TY Lim, b – fivespots. 18 – Eugene Kalenkovich. 19 – shaftinaction. 21 – James van den Broek. 22t – Cathy Keifer, 22l – Nik Bruining, 22b – Pong Wira, 22r – Pong Wira. 23 – guraydere. Images are courtesy of Shutterstock.com. With thanks to Getty Images, Thinkstock Photo and iStockphoto.